20 Answers

❧

Bible
Difficulties

Jimmy Akin

Catholic
Answers
Press

20 Answers: Bible Difficulties

Jimmy Akin

© 2018 Catholic Answers

Published by Catholic Answers, Inc.
2020 Gillespie Way
El Cajon, California 92020
1-888-291-8000 orders
619-387-0042 fax
catholic.com

Printed in the United States of America

978-1-68357-087-5
978-1-68357-088-2 Kindle
978-1-68357-089-9 ePub

Introduction

The books of Scripture firmly, faithfully, and without error teach that truth which God, for the sake of our salvation, wished to see confided to the sacred scriptures (*Dei Verbum* 11).

So said the Second Vatican Council (1962–1965). And the Council was not teaching anything new. The conviction that the books of the Bible teach the truth, that they give us the word of God, has been part of the Christian faith since the very beginning.

Jesus himself declared that "Scripture cannot be broken" (John 10:35), and St. Paul affirmed that "all Scripture is inspired by God" (2 Tim. 3:16).

But not everything in Scripture is easy to understand (cf. Acts 8:30–31; 2 Pet. 3:15–16). Sometimes there are *difficulties*—places where, at least at first glance, it looks like Scripture might be saying something false.

These difficulties come in two kinds. First, there are *internal difficulties*, where one passage of Scripture looks like it might contradict another passage. Second, there are *external difficulties*, where something in Scripture appears to contradict something we know independently, such as a law of science, a fact of history, or a principle of morality.

Since all truth is God's truth, there must be solutions to these difficulties, but why do we encounter them in the first place? Partly it is because of the age in which Scripture was written. Language and culture change over time, creating challenges for us—the citizens of a much later age and culture—when we read ancient writings. Difficulties of this kind can often be cleared up by additional study.

But more fundamentally, it seems to be part of God's providential plan to allow us to wrestle with his word. By doing so, we learn his word even better. This is the way any learning experience works: if a teacher simply tells you the answer to every question as soon as it is posed, you won't learn the material nearly as well as if you studied it on your own, learned to apply key principles, and figured out the answers to problems for yourself.

Learning how to deal with Bible difficulties—both internal and external—is what this short book is about. In the year 405, St. Augustine sketched our general strategy for resolving them:

Of [the canonical scriptures] alone do I most firmly believe that the authors were completely free from error. And if in these writings I am perplexed by anything which appears to me opposed to truth, I do not hesitate to suppose that either the manuscript is faulty, or the translator has not caught the meaning of what was said, or I myself have failed to understand it.[1]

Here Augustine names three ways of dealing with Bible difficulties, by appealing to mistakes made by one of three people:

1. *The Copyist:* In his day, the printing press did not exist, and so every biblical manuscript was hand copied. Unfortunately, scribes were not divinely protected from making mistakes when they copied manuscripts, and so copyist errors are a real phenomenon.

2. *The Translator:* Augustine spoke Latin, and he did not have a good grasp of the languages in which the Bible was written (Hebrew, Aramaic, and Greek). Consequently, like most of us today, he had to use translations. God also did not protect translators from making mistakes, and there have been translation errors in the history of the Bible.

3. *The Interpreter:* Finally, Augustine humbly recognized that God did not protect him—as an interpreter of the Bible—from making mistakes. That's an important admission, and we need to have the humility to make it, too.

In the first part of this book, we will flesh out the principles that Augustine names. After dealing briefly with copyist and translator errors (answers 1 and 2), we will take an in-depth look at the kinds of mistakes that interpreters make (answers 3 through 10).

In the second part (answers 11 through 20), we will apply those principles to key examples of Bible difficulties, and show how they can be resolved. Seeing how the principles can be applied to particular cases will also help you deal with other difficulties not covered in this book.

I hope that you find this effort interesting and informative, that it will help you learn God's word even better, and thus help you grow closer to him.

1. How do copyist errors create Bible difficulties?

If you've ever tried copying a long piece of text by hand, you know how easy it can be to make mistakes.

Since you can only hold a few words or phrases in mind at one time, you have to keep glancing back and forth between the original text and the copy you're making. It's thus easy to lose your place. As you copy the text, you can accidentally omit a word or phrase— or copy it twice.

You also might misspell a word, especially for sound-alike words (for example, "to" instead of "too" or "two"). You might unintentionally say the same thing in slightly different words ("he didn't" instead of "he did not").

You might hit a place where the original is illegible, forcing you to guess at what the writer meant to say.

You might even come across an error made by a *previous* copyist and not be sure how to fix it.

All these problems are common in hand copying, and that was the only kind of copying available before the invention of the printing press in the 1400s.

As the Bible became the most popular book in world history, thousands of copies were produced, but in the age of hand copying this also meant that thousands of tiny copyist errors were created. Each time a copyist made a mistake, it introduced a variant reading into the manuscript he was creating.

Errors have even happened in the age of the printing press. A famous example is the "Adulterous Bible"—an edition of the King James Version that was printed in 1631. When the printers were typesetting the Ten Commandments, they accidentally left out the word "not" so that Exodus 20:14 ended up saying, "Thou shalt commit adultery"!

Sometimes skeptics portray the existence of manuscript variants as a huge problem—as if all the tiny copyist errors rob us of the ability to know what the Bible originally said—but this is not true.

Take the example of the Adulterous Bible. Its famous printer error was spotted because people knew what the Ten Commandments should say based on all the other bibles in circulation—ones that *didn't* have the typo. It was easy to compare the new copies to the old ones and see the problem.

The Bible's popularity—the fact there are thousands of early manuscripts—thus gives us a solution to the problem of copyist errors: if an individual manuscript contains slips of the pen, there are numerous other manuscripts with which we can compare it.

Over the last few centuries, a whole field of scholarship—known as *textual criticism*—has developed to identify the original readings of Bible passages. Scholars have surveyed and catalogued the variations copyists introduced in the early manuscripts, classified them, and developed techniques for identifying what the original readings would have been.

Not every question has been resolved, but textual criticism has made it easy to identify copyist errors. It has also shown that most of these are very minor and that none of them substantially affects Christian doctrine. Although the problem of copyist errors may have been significant in Augustine's day, then, it no longer affects most readers. The development of textual criticism and the invention of the printing press—which allows thousands of identical copies of a Bible to be produced at once—has largely cured it.

A modern reader thus can have great confidence that the Bible in his hands doesn't suffer from this kind of problem. Even when there is a significant variant in the early manuscripts—one that textual criticism hasn't resolved—modern bibles will contain a footnote telling the reader about the variant, allowing him to make up his own mind.

For Bible readers who want to go further in exploring variants, they are discussed in standard commentaries, and everyone is welcome to read the works of textual criticism that scholars have produced and thus assess the evidence for themselves. To do so, however, you'll need to know the languages in which the early manuscripts are written, which brings us to our next subject.

2. How do translation errors create Bible difficulties?

The Italians have a saying: *Traduttore, traditore.* It means "Translator, traitor," and it's a wry reflection on the fact that translation can be hard.

No language maps perfectly onto another one, with all the same meanings and nuances—especially when complex ideas are being translated. Every translator thus, at least in a minor way, "betrays" his source material by not bringing it across fully into the new language. He may be able to bring across the fundamental meaning, but not all the subtleties and connotations.

Here's a famous example: in Greek, the final clause of the Lord's Prayer asks God to deliver us from *tou ponêrou*. In English, you could translate that one of two ways—either "evil" or "the evil one" (i.e., the devil). English doesn't have a way to capture that ambiguity in a single word or phrase, so the translator must make a choice. In doing so, he has to sacrifice the ambiguity that's in the Greek and say something more definite in English.

Translators face this kind of choice even when they are doing their jobs well, but sometimes translators lack skill or are motivated by ideological biases. An example of the latter is the Jehovah's Witnesses' *New World Translation*, which deliberately twists what is in the original languages to fit the group's theology. But although translator mistakes and biases are always possible, modern, mainstream Bible translations keep them to a minimum.

This is possible because the way biblical languages work is well understood, and scholars in every Christian community recognize that their counterparts are doing good, competent work in Bible translation. If a Bible translation appeared that had major problems, these would be quickly spotted by scholars of *every* persuasion, and the translation would be severely critiqued (as the *New World Translation* has been).

Despite the high quality of modern Bible translations, though, the process of translation can still lead to difficulties that puzzle readers.

Consider how the Revised Standard Version (RSV) translates passages in Acts that describe Paul's conversion and what happened when Jesus spoke to him. In one passage, we read, "The men who were traveling with him stood speechless, hearing (*akouontes*) the voice (*phônês*) but seeing no one" (Acts 9:7). In another passage, Paul says, "Now those who were with me saw the light but did not hear (*êkousan*) the voice (*phônên*) of the one who was speaking to me" (Acts 22:9). Both verses have forms of the Greek verb *akouô* for "hear" and the noun *phônê* for "voice." One seems to say that the men with Paul heard the voice and the other that they didn't.

The solution to this seeming contradiction has to do with the meaning of the Greek words. *Akouô* doesn't just mean "hear." If you check a standard Greek dictionary, you'll see it also means "understand." And *phônê* doesn't just mean "voice"; it also means "sound."

Since Luke—the author of Acts—is unlikely to contradict himself in recounting a story he undoubtedly heard from Paul multiple times, the logical thing to do is read the passages in harmony with each other, letting the relevant Greek words have their true range of meanings.

That's what the *New International Version* does in translating these passages: the men traveling with Paul "heard the sound" (Acts 9:7, NIV), but "they did not understand the voice of him who was speaking to me" (Acts 22:9, NIV).

The takeaway for Bible readers is that, when we encounter a Bible difficulty, we should consider whether the problem may be generated by the way the text is being translated. Could there be another translation that would clear up the difficulty? One way to investigate this possibility is to look at other translations and see what they say. Someone puzzled by the way the *Revised Standard Version* translates Acts could consult the *New International Version* and see the solution.

We are blessed today by having a large number of high quality, professional Bible translations, and even if you don't have knowledge of the biblical languages, you can consult other translations and see if they render the text in a way that doesn't produce the difficulty. Some websites (e.g., BibleHub.com) even specialize in showing you the same passage in multiple translations at once.

If you need to dig deeper, you can always consult detailed Bible commentaries or even start studying the biblical languages for yourself.

3. What is the most important question a Bible interpreter needs to ask?

Although Bible difficulties can arise from the process of copying or translating, most of the time the problem is generated when the text is being *interpreted*. In other words, when the interpreter has trouble understanding the text correctly. This was the last of St. Augustine's three sources of difficulties, and it is so common that we will look in detail at different ways it can happen.

Fortunately, there is a central question that can help an interpreter focus his thoughts when trying to resolve a Bible difficulty: what, precisely, is the author of Scripture trying to *assert*?

To understand the importance of this question, we need to look at what the Second Vatican Council says about the way Scripture was written:

> In composing the sacred books, God chose men and while employed by him they made use of their powers and abilities, so that with him acting in them and through them, they, as true authors, consigned to writing everything and only those things which he wanted.
>
> Therefore, since everything asserted by the inspired authors or sacred writers must be held to be asserted by the Holy Spirit, it follows that the books of Scripture must be acknowledged as teaching solidly, faithfully, and without error that truth which God wanted put into sacred writings for the sake of salvation (*Dei Verbum* 11).

We can rephrase the logic of this passage like this:

- Under divine inspiration, the biblical authors wrote everything God wanted and no more.

- Therefore, everything the biblical authors assert is asserted by the Holy Spirit.

- Everything the Holy Spirit asserts is true.

- Therefore, everything the biblical authors assert is true.

This is why it is important, when resolving a Bible difficulty, to determine what the biblical author is asserting. But that task is not always easy. Sometimes we think that the biblical author is asserting something that he isn't. This is a particular danger since the biblical texts were written centuries ago and in a different culture.

In 1943, Pope Pius XII commented,

> What is the literal sense of a passage is not always as obvious in the speeches and writings of the ancient authors of the East, as it is in the works of our own time. For what they wished to express is not to be determined by the rules of grammar and philology alone, nor solely by the context; the interpreter must, as it were, go back wholly in spirit to those remote centuries of the East and with the aid of history, archaeology, ethnology, and other sciences, to accurately determine what modes of writing, so to speak, the authors of that ancient period would be likely to use, and in fact did use.

> For the ancient peoples of the East, in order to express their ideas, did not always employ those forms or kinds of speech which we use today; but rather those used by the men of their times and countries. What those exactly were the commentator cannot

determine as it were in advance, but only after a careful examination of the ancient literature of the East (*Divino Afflante Spiritu* 35–36).

The difference in time and culture between the biblical age and ours can make it difficult for modern interpreters to determine what the authors of the Bible were asserting, and when they get this wrong, Bible difficulties can result. To resolve these difficulties, therefore, we have to figure out what the authors were asserting and what they were not.

For example, early Christians often assumed that the Second Coming of Jesus would occur within their own lifetimes. St. Paul seems to assume this when he writes, "We who are alive, who are left, shall be caught up together with them in the clouds to meet the Lord in the air" (1 Thess. 4:17). Yet Jesus did not return in Paul's life.

This would be a problem if Paul had indeed asserted that Jesus *would*. In that case, Scripture would be wrong. But that isn't what's happening in this passage. Paul may be tentatively *assuming* that Jesus would return quickly, but he isn't *asserting* it. The point he is asserting is that those who are alive at the Second Coming (whoever they may be) will be caught up to be with Jesus. Elsewhere Paul expresses doubt that he would remain alive (Phil. 2:17), and by the end of his career he was certain he would die (2 Tim. 4:6–8).

Being sensitive to the difference between a definite assertion and a tentative assumption allows us to resolve this potential difficulty, and similar techniques will allow us to resolve others.

4. Why is genre important?

The word *genre* refers to a type of composition. Genres occur in every kind of media: classical and hip-hop are genres of music; sitcoms and news programs are genres of television; westerns and science fiction are genres of movies; and so on.

Each work in a genre is composed according to certain conventions or rules, which define the genre. Classical music uses orchestral instruments, whereas hip-hop uses synthesizers and record sampling. Sitcoms use laugh tracks, but news programs don't. Westerns have cowboys and horses, and science fiction has aliens and space ships. Sometimes you even find works that fuse two genres, such as sci-fi westerns, which feature both cowboys and aliens.

In written literature, there are many genres, and that also applies to the literature in the Bible. Originally, the Bible was not a single book but a collection of books written in different genres. Some of them contain biographies (the Gospels), some histories (1–2 Samuel, Acts), some hymns (the Psalms), some prophesies and visions (Isaiah, Revelation), some wise sayings (Proverbs, Sirach), some laws (Leviticus, Deuteronomy), and some are letters (Romans, 1–2 Corinthians).

Individual books of the Bible also can fuse different genres. Thus the Gospels contain not only biographical information about what Jesus did and what happened to him in his life, they also contain his teaching, which is expressed in a variety of genres, including ethical discourse (Matt. 5–7), parables (Matt. 13), and prophecy (Matt. 24–25).

When interpreting the Bible, it is important to identify the genre that a biblical author is using and to understand the rules by which that genre works. If you don't know those things, Bible difficulties are sure to result.

For example, prophecies and parables make heavy use of symbolism in their narratives, but historical narratives generally don't. It would be a mistake to read Revelation 13 and conclude that John means that a literal seven-headed beast will literally rise out of the sea and begin persecuting Christians. It also would be a mistake to read Jesus' parable of the sower (Matt. 13:3–9) and conclude that he was telling a story about a real, namable farmer who lived in his own day.

The rules that different genres obey are like rules of grammar: they help the author communicate his meaning to the audience, and if you don't understand the rules, you won't be able to figure out what the author is asserting and what he isn't. As Pius XII indicated (answer 3), we can't determine the rules of a genre in advance. Instead, we need to make "a careful examination of the ancient literature of the East" (*Divino Afflante Spiritu*).

When reading the Bible, we must be sensitive to small cues in the text that can help us identify the genre we are reading and the rules that it obeys, because it can sometimes be difficult for a modern reader to figure this out.

For example, some modern readers look at the book of Judith and assume it is a work of history. This immediately generates a difficulty, as the first verse describes Nebuchadnezzar as the king of the Assyrians. "But," some say, "everybody knows that Nebuchadnezzar was the king of the Babylonians, not the Assyrians!" And yes, that's the point: everybody *did* know this. The first verse deliberately combines the two great enemies of Israel (the Babylonians and the Assyrians).

As you keep reading, you discover the book is about a conflict between one of Nebuchadnezzar's generals and Judith, a heroine whose name means "Lady Jew" and who thus personifies the Jewish people.

The effect is as if a modern person read a story that pitted Miss America against a general sent by Adolph Hitler, leader of the USSR, thus combining America's two great opponents of the twentieth century—the Nazis and the Soviets. The content of the book—right from the first verse—thus signals to the reader that he isn't reading a historical work but a kind of extended parable. Identifying the genre of Judith thus clears up the historical difficulties that would otherwise result.

Another example of how understanding genre is important is found in the book of Proverbs. Sometimes people confuse proverbs with laws, and if you do that, problems will result. For example, Proverbs 26:4 says, "Answer not a fool according to his folly, lest you be like him yourself." But the next verse says, "Answer a fool according to his folly, lest he be wise in his own eyes."

If these were laws that always had to be obeyed, there would be a problem, because they conflict. But they are not laws. They are proverbs, or wise sayings. By juxtaposing the two sayings, the author of Proverbs is telling us that *sometimes* it is wise not to answer a fool in kind, but *sometimes* it is. Rather than always doing one or the other, we need to use our prudential judgment to determine which is the wise course of action in a particular case.

5. What role does approximation play?

We live in a detail-oriented age. People today like exact records and precise measurements.

There is even a whole field—known as *metrology*—devoted to the scientific study of measurement. It allows us to say things like, "The speed of light in a vacuum is 186,282 miles per second," and, "The average atomic weight of an iron atom is 55.845."

Although this degree of precision is useful in some circumstances, we don't use anything like it in everyday life. Most of the time, we have no need for it, and it would actually get in the way if we had to specify everything down to the last decimal place.

Consequently, when we describe things we normally use *approximations*. We say, "It rained a lot yesterday," not, "There was 4.781 inches of precipitation yesterday." It would be absurd to expect people to use scientific levels of precision when an approximation would allow them to make their basic point.

Ancient people also used approximations. Indeed, they had to, because metrology and scientific measurement hadn't been invented yet. For many things, approximations were all they had—but they were all they needed to communicate their message.

Understanding this plays a role in resolving Bible difficulties, because to grasp what a biblical author is asserting, you need to know what degree of approximation he was using.

For example, some have seen a difficulty in the measurements the Bible gives for the metal basin or "sea" used for ceremonial washings in Solomon's temple. Scripture says it was ten cubits across, and "a line of thirty cubits measured its circumference" (1 Kings 7:23; 2 Chron. 4:2). That would imply that the value of π (*pi*) is 3, which is too small. π is an irrational number slightly greater than 3.14159, and the sea should have had a circumference of more than thirty-one cubits.

This example involves expecting a modern, scientific degree of approximation when it's not appropriate. The difficulty vanishes when you realize the biblical author wasn't asserting that the sea had a diameter of *exactly* ten cubits and a circumference of *exactly* thirty cubits. He was just approximating, the same way a modern person likely would in ordinary speech.

Approximation doesn't occur just when numbers are involved. It also occurs when words are involved, and difficulties arise if you don't recognize this. Many have seen Bible difficulties in the fact that the Gospels sometimes phrase things Jesus said in different ways or report him giving long speeches that would not have been memorized at the time.

But suppose that, today, you are telling a co-worker about something your boss said. Unless you tape-recorded your boss or took shorthand dictation, you probably won't use his exact words. Instead, you'll give an approximation of what he said. You'll express the same meaning, but you'll use somewhat different words to convey it: a *paraphrase*.

In the ancient world, they didn't have tape recorders, and knowledge of shorthand was rare. This meant that, whenever one person quoted another, it was almost always a paraphrase. The only exceptions—also rare—were when one person made a deliberate effort to memorize something someone said in a word-for-word fashion.

In the case of a great teacher, someone might make the effort to memorize his sayings. Some of Jesus' sayings are short and vivid and structured in a way that would aid memorization, such as "the last will be first, and the first last" (Matt. 20:16). But paraphrases were the norm, and even sayings like that one could be paraphrased (see Matt. 19:30, Mark 10:31, Luke 13:30). If a stranger came up to Jesus and asked to be healed, nobody would expect the disciples to memorize *exactly* what the person said or what Jesus replied. When the event was recounted later, the audience would have expected the disciples (including the biblical author) to approximate what was said.

One thing we often do when paraphrasing is to flesh out the implications of what a person said and cover them in more detail. The ancients did that, too, and this is the likely explanation for the long speeches in John's Gospel. As an eyewitness (John 21:24), John knew Jesus and understood his thought intimately, allowing him to flesh out its meaning even when reporting one-time speeches that he would not have memorized on the spot.

6. How did the biblical authors select which facts to record?

Modern printing technology has made it possible to print lengthy books very cheaply. Today you can buy a 2,000-page Bible for twenty dollars or less.

This is not the way it was in the ancient world. Back then, when you had to pay scribes to write out every copy of a book by hand, books were fantastically expensive, and only the rich could afford them. Furthermore, books didn't have square spines the way modern books do. Instead, they were written on scrolls that you had to roll and unroll as you read them.

Both these facts meant books were smaller. Virtually nobody could afford a 2,000-page book, and absolutely nobody would want to roll through a 2,000-page scroll! Considerations of affordability and usability therefore led authors to keep their works concise. That's why you can read an individual Gospel, an ancient biography of Jesus, in just two or three hours.

But Jesus lived for more than thirty years, and his ministry lasted for more than three. If an ancient author wanted to write Jesus' biography, he would have to be very selective in what material he decided to include. That's why John closes his Gospel by saying, "But there are also many other things which Jesus did; were every one of them to be written, I suppose that the world itself could not contain the books that would be written" (John 21:25).

When modern people don't recognize the need for biblical authors to be selective in choosing what details to include, it can lead to Bible difficulties.

For example, sometimes one Gospel will tell of an incident and mention it involving a single individual, whereas another Gospel will mention it involving two. Thus Mark 5:2 tells of Jesus exorcizing a single demoniac, but Matthew 8:28 mentions two demoniacs. Similarly, in Matthew 28:2 there is mention of one angel announcing Jesus' resurrection at his tomb, whereas in Luke 24:4 there are two.

Some have seen these as contradictions, but they are not. The authors are simply making different choices in which details to record. In reality, there were two demoniacs who were exorcized, and there were two angels at the tomb. One author mentions this, while another omits the detail and shortens the report to its essentials.

Different choices regarding which details to include can manifest in other ways. For example, Matthew records that a centurion asked Jesus to heal his son (Matt. 8:5–13), while Luke mentions the detail that the request was made through intermediaries rather than in person (Luke 7:1–10).

We see different choices being made in which details to include in theological discussions also. For example, in the Sermon on the Mount, Jesus says, "Let your light so shine before men, that they may see your good works and give glory to your Father who is in heaven" (Matt. 5:16). But a little later, he says, "Beware of practicing your piety before men in order to be seen by them; for then you will have no reward from your Father who is in heaven" (Matt. 6:1).

By placing both of these sayings in the same context,

Matthew is not contradicting himself. He expects us to read them both and to understand them in harmony with each other. Each expresses part of the truth but not the whole truth: we *should* let others see our good works when it would help them glorify God, but we *should not* do so out of a desire to glorify ourselves.

Making decisions about which facts to include on which occasions is something we do all the time. We almost never give technical, exhaustive statements of what we know about a subject. Instead, we mention certain facts on certain occasions, as determined by what we need to communicate at the moment. We then expect others to understand such partial statements in harmony with each other.

The biblical authors did the same things. They chose which facts to include based on what they were trying to communicate. Sometimes they mentioned more details to communicate a fuller message. Sometimes they mentioned fewer in order to save space or communicate more simply. By recognizing this and reading their statements in harmony with each other, we can resolve many Bible difficulties.

7. How did the biblical authors sequence their material?

Think about a time several years ago when you had pizza for dinner. Now think about another time, also several years ago, when you had pasta. Got them both in mind?

Let me ask you a question: which occasion occurred first?

Odds are, you won't be able to say. Unless you have a freakishly detailed memory, or unless you keep detailed food logs, you won't be able to recall the exact dates or the sequence in which these events happened. You can certainly remember occasions of eating pizza and pasta since our memories are good enough to preserve the essence of these experiences, but the knowledge of precisely when they happened fades quickly.

Ancient authors—both biblical and secular—had memories that worked the same way. Unless someone made a written, chronological record of an event, they would remember *what* happened, but not precisely *when* it happened. This meant that they would have to make choices about the sequence in which they presented their material.

For example, in *The Lives of the Twelve Caesars* by the Roman historian Suetonius, the biographies have a kind of loose chronological structure: they begin with an account of the caesar's family history and early life; they cover his rise to power; and they end with an account of the caesar's death and legacy.

But in the middle, things can be organized in a non-chronological way. Suetonius frequently groups the *positive* things a caesar did in office in one section, and he recounts the *negative* things the same caesar did in another section.

We find something similar in the Gospels: they also have a loose chronological structure, beginning (in Matthew and Luke's case) with his birth, covering his baptism by John and the beginning of his ministry, recounting the growth of his popularity (as illustrated by events like the feeding of the 5,000), and concluding with his death and resurrection. That's the natural structure of his life and ministry, and all the Gospels reflect it.

But apart from these key events, the Gospels vary the order in which they relate what Jesus said and did. Some people have noticed that and accused the Gospels of contradicting each other.

The solution to this difficulty is recognizing that the biblical authors—like other ancient authors—were not trying to give a strictly chronological account. Sometimes they used chronology, which is why they all record Jesus' baptism before his death. Sometimes they even give us very specific chronological information (such as in Luke 3:1–3).

But other times they arranged material by different criteria, such as by topic. Matthew's Gospel provides very clear examples of this. In Mark and Luke, we find sayings of Jesus scattered in many places, but Matthew gathers the same sayings up and groups them together by topic. He has Jesus' major ethical teachings in the Sermon on the Mount (Matt. 5–7), he has Jesus' major parables in a single discourse (Matt. 13), and he has Jesus' prophecies in the Olivet Discourse (Matt. 24–25).

By adopting a topical arrangement for Jesus' sayings, Matthew is doing essentially the same thing that Suetonius did in grouping together the good and bad acts of the different caesars. Ancient readers knew that authors wrote in this manner, sometimes arranging material chronologically and sometimes topically, and we need to understand this, too.

If we don't, we may falsely conclude that the biblical authors are *asserting* that the events they record happened in a particular sequence, when in fact they aren't. They are asserting *that* something was said or done, but often they aren't asserting anything about precisely *when* it happened. An awareness of the way biblical authors sequenced their material thus clears up many potential Bible difficulties.

8. How are different modes of speech important?

We use figures of speech all the time, without even realizing it. They are part of how we naturally think. But if we stop to analyze what we say, they leap out at us.

For example, the previous paragraph contains an example of a figure of speech known as *hyperbole*, or exaggeration to make a point. It isn't literally true that we use figures of speech *all the time*—without any interruption whatsoever. You know that, yet you also know what I meant.

The ancients, including the biblical authors, did the same thing. But because their culture was different from ours, we may not recognize the figures of speech they used.

Sometimes our bibles render the stranger expressions in idiomatic English. For example, in the RSV, Exodus 34:6 says that God is "slow to anger." What it literally says in Hebrew is that God is "long of nose." Being long of nose was a Hebrew figure of speech for being patient.

Other times, modern bibles leave it up to the reader to identify and interpret non-literal modes of speech. Sometimes recognizing them is easy. We all know that prophetic books like Revelation contain a large number of symbols and that Jesus' parables aren't meant to be accounts of historical incidents. We may still have to work to figure out what they mean, but we recognize that they aren't intended to be taken literally.

In some cases, however, it isn't so easy to spot non-literal speech in the Bible, and that can lead to Bible difficulties. For example, Mormons sometimes appeal to passages that refer to God's "outstretched arm" or his all-seeing eyes (Deut. 4:34, Prov. 15:3) as evidence for their view that God is an "exalted man." But elsewhere the Bible forthrightly states that God is "not a man" (Num. 23:19; 1 Sam. 15:29).

They key to resolving this difficulty is recognizing that the former passages are not meant literally. They involve a figure of speech known as *anthropomorphic language*—that is, language that depicts something (or someone, in this case God) as *if it* were human. The literal truth is that God is not a man, but the biblical authors use human symbols like arms and eyes to convey a sense of his power and knowledge.

Difficulties can also arise when a person fails to recognize a mode of figurative speech known as *phenomenological language*, which describes phenomena according to their appearances. For example, some passages in Scripture speak of the dead as being asleep (Ps. 13:3, Dan. 12:2, Matt. 9:24), but others indicate that the dead are conscious in the afterlife (Luke 16:19–31; 2 Cor. 5:8; Rev. 6:9–11, 7:13–15).

The solution is that the former passages describe the condition of the dead based on appearances—they *appear* to be asleep (they don't stand up, don't move around, and typically have their eyes closed). But in reality their souls are conscious and with God.

Another famous example of phenomenological language in the Bible is references to the sun rising and setting (Ps. 113:3, Eccles. 1:5, Isa. 45:6)—figures of speech that we still use today.

Finally, Bible difficulties can be generated when we fail to appreciate a concept known as the *universe of discourse* (also known as the domain of discourse).

This refers to the range of things that are under discussion. For example, in Romans 3:23, Paul says that "all have sinned." This would create a problem if Paul was speaking absolutely. In that case, both Jesus and Mary would be counted as sinners.

But Paul is not discussing them. He has a restricted universe of discourse, as can be shown by the fact that later in the same letter he refers to unborn children who have not sinned (Rom. 9:11). Paul is discussing ordinary individuals, not people who aren't old enough to make moral choices, like infants, or who have a special place in God's plan, like Jesus and Mary (cf. Heb. 4:15).

9. Why is identifying the author's attitude important?

Bible difficulties often come up when people do not correctly discern the biblical author's attitude toward what he is describing. If we fail to do this, we may conclude that the Bible is endorsing something when it is not.

Scripture records people committing many violent and sinful actions, for example, and some biblical critics charge that it must be endorsing the things that it depicts. However, this is not the case.

Consider an obvious example: Scripture sometimes quotes the devil (e.g., Job 1:9–10, Matt. 4:3, 6, 9). Obviously, the biblical authors do not endorse things said by Satan. Indeed, they acknowledge that he "has nothing to do with the truth, because there is no truth in him. When he lies, he speaks according to his own nature, for he is a liar and the father of lies" (John 8:44).

This presents us with an important caution against taking biblical passages out of context. Just because the Bible reports something, that doesn't mean it approves of it. In fact, the biblical author may be doing just the opposite, as in the case of Satan.

That's a particularly obvious example, but the principle holds in other cases, and even with Israel's leaders. In the literature of some ancient peoples, rulers are consistently portrayed in a positive light. In Egypt, for example, pharaohs were always depicted as winning battles, never as losing them.

By contrast, the Old Testament historical books are remarkably frank about the defeats and flaws of the Hebrew kings. In fact, among ancient authors the men who wrote the Bible were uniquely straightforward about the sins of their kings, and even offer a critique of the institution of kingship itself, pointing out the abuses to which monarchy can lead (see 1 Sam. 8:10–18).

This applies even for kings with otherwise good reputations, such as David. Thus Scripture doesn't shy from reporting David's seduction of Bathsheba, the wife of another man. This could have been portrayed positively, as an act illustrating the king's machismo and his skillful outmaneuvering of a lesser man. But the biblical author presents it as sinful. He further reports that when Bathsheba becomes pregnant, David tries to avoid responsibility. He first tries to convince her husband that he is actually the father and, when this fails, he arranges for him to be killed in battle. God then sends a prophet to denounce David for his actions and proclaim judgment upon him (2 Sam. 11–12).

Sometimes the biblical authors convey their disapproval even without recording an explicit divine judgment on the man in question. This happens in the case of the judge Jephthah, who foolishly and immorally makes a vow, if he is victorious in battle, to sacrifice the first person to come out of his home.

The biblical author then lets the horrific consequences of this act speak for themselves when Jephthah's only child—his beloved daughter—comes out to celebrate her father's victory, and he feels compelled to keep his vow. The author portrays all this matter-of-factly, without explicitly condemning Jephthah, but he notes that this became the basis of a yearly observance of mourning what happened to his daughter (Judg. 11).

This kind of reportage is similar to modern accounts in which a news reporter or historian relates events in a straightforward way and allows the character of what happened to speak for itself, without offering editorial comment. Modern authors may expect their audience to recognize that something was bad without stopping to say, "And this was wrong," and biblical authors do the same thing.

The biblical authors were, however, men of their own day, and their attitudes reflect this fact. In some cases, they held attitudes that would later be supplemented and corrected by further revelation. In these cases, they may view incidents more positively or leniently than we would today, which brings us to our next point.

10. What role does progressive revelation play?

The Bible was written over a period of around a thousand years. The first books of the Old Testament were written around the time of King David, or perhaps a few centuries earlier, and the last books of the Bible—those of the New Testament—were written in the first century A.D.

This means that God did not give his revelation all at once. As the *Catechism of the Catholic Church* (CCC) says, "God has revealed himself to man by gradually communicating his own mystery in deeds and in words" (68). Theologians refer to this gradual process as *progressive revelation*.

One consequence of progressive revelation is that people living in earlier ages did not have all of the information that those living in later ages did. This is why some passages in the Old Testament do not clearly envision the resurrection of the dead. The Israelites, like people of every culture, believed in an afterlife, but the specific form of the afterlife, involving resurrection, was only revealed gradually (CCC 992).

The progressive nature of revelation has other implications. In 2010, Pope Benedict XVI explained,

> God's plan is manifested progressively, and it is accomplished slowly, in successive stages and despite human resistance. God chose a people and patiently worked to guide and educate them. Revelation is suited to the cultural and moral level of distant times and thus describes facts and customs, such as cheating and trickery, and acts of violence and massacre, without explicitly denouncing the immorality of such things. This can be explained by the historical context, yet it can cause the modern reader to be taken aback, especially if he or she fails to take account of the many "dark" deeds carried out down the centuries, and also in our own day. In the Old Testament, the preaching of the prophets vigorously challenged every kind of injustice and violence, whether collective or individual, and thus became God's way of training his people in preparation for the gospel (*Verbum Domini* 42).

One aspect of God's progressive revelation is that he was initially willing to tolerate certain things because of human weakness, and then gradually showed his people a better way, ultimately revealing the fullness of his will in the example of Jesus Christ.

Thus Jesus indicated that God initially tolerated divorce because the Israelites were stubbornly attached to the institution: "For your hardness of heart [Moses] wrote you this commandment" (Mark 10:5). Jesus then gave the full revelation of God's will: "What therefore God has joined together, let not man put asunder" (Mark 10:9).

Parents may tolerate behavior from a small child that they would not allow once the child has matured, and in the same way, God allowed the early Israelites to do things that—by the time of Jesus—he revealed were not his will. This is a recurring theme in Jesus' teaching, as when he says, "You have heard that it was said, 'An eye for an eye and a tooth for a tooth.' But I say to you, do not resist one who is evil. But if any one strikes you on the right cheek, turn to him the other also" (Matt. 5:38–39).

This principle of God tolerating things temporarily as he leads people toward moral and spiritual maturity applies even in our own lives (cf. 2 Cor. 10:5b–6), and it explains many Bible difficulties involving the harsher laws in the Old Testament.

These laws were based on the harsh culture that prevailed when God first began working with the Israelites, and over time he gradually corrected them, ultimately revealing the ethic of love even for one's enemies (Matt. 5:44), as demonstrated when Jesus willingly went to the cross and prayed that those who executed him would be forgiven (Luke 23:34).

11. Does Genesis contradict modern science?

The first chapter of Genesis contains a creation narrative in which God is depicted as creating the world in a period of seven days. This is markedly different from the proposals made by scientists, who point to evidence that the universe and life developed gradually, over a period of billions of years.

Some have proposed that this difficulty can be resolved by the fact the Hebrew word for *day* (*yom*) can refer either to a twenty-four-hour period or to a longer period of time. The latter use is present even in English. We sometimes use *day* to refer to historical periods—for example, "Conditions were different in Napoleon's day." Some thus have proposed that the days of Genesis 1 could refer to periods of time that were billions of years long.

There are two problems with this view. First, even if it were true, it would not harmonize with the findings of science; for Genesis 1 depicts the birds being created before the land animals (vv. 20–25), yet paleontology indicates it was the other way around. Second, the text depicts the days as twenty-four-hour periods, for each is divided into "evening" and "morning" (vv. 5, 8, 13,

19, 23, 31), so either they are literal twenty-four-hour days or they are non-literal symbols.

A better solution to the difficulty is found when we pay careful attention to the text of Genesis itself. A close reading reveals that, despite what one might initially think, the text is not attempting to give us chronological information about the origin of the world. Instead, as the *Catechism* points out, it presents "the work of the Creator symbolically as a succession of six days of divine 'work'" (337).

The symbolism is revealed by the way the passage is structured. Initially, we are told that "In the beginning God created the heavens and the earth" (v. 1) and "The earth was without form and void" (v. 2)—in other words, it was unstructured and empty.

Over the first three days, God solves the formlessness problem by giving structure to the world: on day one he separates day from night; on day two he separates sky from sea; and on day three he separates the waters of the sea so that dry land appears (vv. 3–13).

Having solved the formlessness problem, God then solves the emptiness problem, and over the next three days he goes back over the same realms—in the same order—and populates them: on day four he populates the day and the night with the sun, moon, and stars; on day five he populates the sky and sea with the birds and the fish; and on day six he populates the land with the animals and man (vv. 14–31).

Once the earth is no longer formless and empty, God rests on the seventh day (2:1–3).

For our purposes, it's important to note that the sun is not created until the fourth day. The ancients knew just as well as we that the presence or absence of the sun is what causes the day/night cycle. The creation of the sun on the fourth day is thus a signal to the audience that the text is not meant to be taken literally but symbolically: it fits the work of the Creator into the framework of a Hebrew week, telling us *what* God did, but without intending to give us literal, chronological information about *when* God did it. Instead, it arranges the material *topically*, as God progressively solves the problems of formlessness and emptiness.

The difficulty is thus solved by careful attention to the genre of the text (answer 4), to the sequencing of the material in a topical rather than chronological fashion (answer 7), and to the text's use of non-literal language (answer 8).

Consequently, John Paul II noted,

Above all, this text has a religious and theological importance. It doesn't contain significant elements from the point of view of the natural sciences. Research on the origin and development of the individual species in nature does not find in this description any definitive norm or positive contributions of substantial interest. Indeed, the theory of natural evolution, understood in a sense that does not exclude divine causality, is not in principle opposed to the truth about the creation of the visible world, as presented in the book of Genesis.[2]

12. Is Genesis based on pagan narratives?

In the nineteenth century, archaeologists began to translate the literature of a number of ancient peoples, including the Egyptians, Babylonians, and Sumerians. As they did so, they discovered a variety of accounts that have similarities to the early chapters of Genesis. They contain creation narratives, flood stories, and so forth.

Strikingly, some of these accounts were written earlier than Genesis was. Most scholars hold that the material in Genesis was written sometime between the tenth and eighth centuries B.C., though some scholars say it was a few centuries earlier. Given the similarities between the texts, the question of the extent to which the author of Genesis borrowed from them was certain to arise.

From a Catholic perspective, the idea that the text of Genesis was in some way influenced by these accounts does not create a Bible difficulty. As Pope Pius XII explained,

If, however, the ancient sacred writers have taken anything from popular narrations (and this may be conceded), it must never be forgotten that they did so with the help of divine inspiration, through which they were rendered immune from any error in selecting and evaluating those documents (*Humani Generis* 38).

The idea that Genesis would be influenced by such texts should not be surprising. The Israelites were surrounded by powerful civilizations, and they were in contact with the oral traditions and literature of those peoples. It would be natural for Israelites to want to know how to respond to the claims made by their neighbors. We thus find the author of Genesis offering a critique of pagan views, and this critique manifests in a number of ways.

For example, although Genesis 1 describes God creating the sun and the moon (vv. 14–18), it never uses the Hebrew words for these bodies. Instead, it describes them simply as "lights" and explains that their function is "to give light upon the earth" and to provide ways of reckoning "for signs and for seasons and for days and years."

The reason the author does this is to correct the pagan view that the sun and the moon were deities. That's why he never uses their names: the Hebrew words for *sun* and *moon* were the names of the Canaanite solar and lunar deities, and the author wants to avoid the idea that God was the creator of a pantheon that included the sun and moon gods. Thus he describes them simply as lights and describes their functions. The message is: *they're not gods; don't worship them!*

Pagan narratives typically focused on the creation of a pantheon of gods, often by sexual reproduction, and they sometimes presented the creation of the world as due to a violent conflict among the gods. For example, in the Babylonian *Enuma Elish*, the god Marduk tears apart the corpse of the primordial mother goddess Tiamat to make the heavens and the earth. Then Marduk kills Tiamat's husband Kingu and fashions mankind from his blood as a slave race to free the gods from their labor.

A related work known as the *Atrahasis Epic* agrees that men were created so that the gods wouldn't have to work, but it says that men made so much noise that it disturbed the gods' sleep, and it was decided to wipe them out with a great flood.

By contrast, Genesis reveals that the world was created by a single God, and that it was not done in a sexual manner. God merely spoke, and reality obeyed. Creation did not involve a conflict between gods, and it resulted in a good and beautiful world that God entrusted to man.

Furthermore, God did not create man to get out of doing work. Instead, he put man in paradise and gave him the dignified task of stewarding his Creation. We only experience suffering and drudgery because we sinned and rebelled against the role God had given us

(Gen. 3:16–19). Similarly, disasters like the Flood are brought about by human sin (Gen. 6:5–8).

Genesis thus presents a theological vision according to which the world is created and ruled by a single, supreme God, who is good, generous, and just—not a pantheon of squabbling, selfish godlings.

Rather than saying Genesis is "based on" or "borrows from" pagan accounts, it would be more accurate to say that Genesis *responds to* and *corrects* pagan ideas so that we have a true theological understanding of God and his Creation.

13. How should we understand violence in the Old Testament?

We have already noted that Scripture's reporting of people doing violent and immoral things does not mean that it approves of them (answer 9). What are we to make, however, of passages where God seems to command the use of violence in ways that we today would regard as unacceptable? For example, what are we to make of passages where God seems to command the extermination of groups of Canaanite people (Deut. 7:1–2; 20:16–17)?

There are two basic ways of taking these passages: literally and non-literally.

In prior centuries, many interpreters took them as literal commands given by God that the Israelites were expected to carry out. According to this view, the commands were based both on the need to administer justice and to protect against future crimes.

The commands were seen as involving justice:

> According to what is attested in the Bible, the Canaanites are seen by God as guilty of very serious crimes (Gen. 15:16; Lev. 18:3, 24–30; 20:23; Deut. 9:4–5, etc.), among which is the killing of their own children in perverted rituals (Deut. 12:31; 18:10–12). The narrative, then, holds out the prospect of the execution of divine justice in history.[3]

The commands were seen as protecting against future offenses because the text indicates that if these groups remained, they would corrupt the Israelites with their immoral practices (Deut. 7:4; 20:18). The danger of this was seen as so severe that, given the conditions in the ancient world, the only effective way to prevent it was extermination. In fact, the Israelites were later corrupted by the Canaanites and adopted immoral and perverted practices from them, including child sacrifice (cf. 2 Kings 16:3; 17:8, 17, 19; 21:2, 6, 11; Ps. 106:37). This, in turn, caused God's judgment to fall on Israel (2 Chron. 36:14–21).

Even taking these factors into account, moderns may ask how God could give such commands, as they would have involved the deaths of at least some innocent people.

Advocates of the literal view have argued that all life is a gift from God. We do not have a right to it. God has a right to determine how much of that gift we receive and when and how it ends. Thus St. Thomas Aquinas writes,

All men alike, both guilty and innocent, die the death of nature: which death of nature is inflicted by the power of God on account of original sin, according to 1 Samuel 2:6: "The Lord kills and makes alive." Consequently, by the command of God, death can be inflicted on any man, guilty or innocent, without any injustice whatever.[4]

Furthermore, death is not the end. Whatever the circumstances of a particular death, it is a finite evil. Eternity lies before us, and God is capable of more than compensating innocent people who have suffered or died (cf. Rom. 8:18; 2 Cor. 4:17–18).

Advocates of the literal view would thus say that, although the actions God commanded regarding the Canaanites are not for our day, they did not involve injustice.

Some of the Church Fathers, though—and many modern interpreters—have taken these verses in a different sense. According to their view, God did not literally expect the Israelites to exterminate certain Canaanite groups.

Part of the case for this view is based on the fact that the commands are recorded in books written *after* the events in question. For example, the ones cited above are from the book of Deuteronomy, which largely consists of material attributed to Moses. However, though it may contain material that dates to the time of Moses, the book was not completed until later. This is illustrated by the fact that it contains an account of Moses' death and that it indicates a significant period of time has passed (Deut. 34:10–12).

Consequently, the passages concerning the extermination of the Canaanites may not have been composed until after Moses' day. If these commands had post-Mosaic origins then they were not intended to be carried out literally, for Israel was already living in the land. In that case, they would have been meant to communicate a spiritual lesson.

Though it is not a body of the Church's Magisterium, the Pontifical Biblical Commission expresses this view when it writes,

As the best interpreters of the Patristic tradition [i.e., the Church Fathers] had already suggested, the narration of the conquest epic should be seen as a sort of parable presenting characters of symbolic value; the law of extermination, for its part, requires a nonliteral interpretation, as in the case of the command of the Lord to cut off one's hand or pluck out one's eye, if they are a cause of scandal (Matt. 5:29; 18:9).[5]

What could have been the message symbolically communicated by the commands to exterminate certain Canaanite groups? As we've seen, the portrait of the Canaanites is one of great depravity and even involved child sacrifice. By contrast, the Israelites were called to holiness, for they are "a people holy to the Lord" (Deut. 7:6; 14:2; cf. Lev. 11:44; 20:26). The extermination commands may thus be a way of signifying the radical incompatibility of paganism and serving God: paganism is to be entirely avoided, though this does not mean literal extermination any more than Christ meant we should literally cut off our hand to avoid sin.

If this interpretation is correct, the difficulty is resolved by paying careful attention to what the author is and is not asserting (answer 3) and recognizing the role of non-literal speech in his narrative (answer 8). Thus, whether the passages concerning the Canaanites are meant to be taken literally or non-literally, the difficulties they give rise to can be resolved.

14. How should we understand harsh laws in the Old Testament?

The Old Testament contains various laws that do not accord with modern sensibilities, which can generate Bible difficulties. There are a number of ways of resolving these.

First, just because modern sensibilities do not like something does not mean that it must be false. The idea that our ideas today are automatically superior to those of the ancient world reflects a form of *chronological snobbery*; it needs to be asked whether the *modern* ideas are the problematic ones. Compared to people in the ancient world, we lead very soft and comfortable lives, and it is reasonable to ask whether some of our views may have consequently become unrealistic or even degenerate.

Second, we should recognize that many of the laws in question are found in the Pentateuch (the books of Genesis through Deuteronomy) and that they thus reflect an earlier stage of progressive revelation. Jesus indicated that Moses gave the Israelites some laws only because of the hardness of their hearts (Mark 10:5). God was willing to tolerate certain practices among the Israelites for a time, though he ultimately revealed the fullness of his will through Christ (answer 10). The difficulty caused by a particular law thus may be due to the fact it represents something God was tolerating since the Israelites had not yet reached a more advanced stage of cultural and spiritual development.

Third, a careful reading of the legal texts shows that, rather than implying an endorsement, the law was actually trying to limit the damage caused in a situation. For example, some have been shocked by the regulations saying what Israelite men should do when they have captured women in battle and wish to marry them (Deut. 21:10–14), but the purpose of this law actually is to restrain what the men would otherwise do and to provide protections for the captive women.

Thus the men are not allowed to marry the women immediately. There is a waiting period in which the woman makes herself unattractive and mourns for her parents, giving the man a chance to reconsider (vv. 12–13). The text warns the man who still insists on marrying such a woman that he has "humiliated her" (v. 14), and if he decides to divorce her then she has the right to go wherever she wants, including back to her own people. He is not allowed to sell her or treat her as a slave. The text thus seeks to restrain the way the Israelites treated captive women.

Fourth, we should seek to understand the principles on which the laws were based. For example, many moderns criticize harsh-sounding Old Testament statements that speak of taking "an eye for an eye and a tooth for a tooth," but, properly understood, the passages expressed a principle of justice and sought to promote the common good.

Three passages mention the "eye for an eye" principle: Exodus 21:22–25, Leviticus 24:17–21, and Deuteronomy 19:16–21. The first deals with the case of men who are fighting and accidentally injure a pregnant woman, causing miscarriage. The second deals with a man who attacks and maims another. The third deals with a witness who lies in court to harm an innocent person. In each passage a similar formula occurs: "you shall give life for life, eye for eye, tooth for tooth, hand for hand, foot for foot, burn for burn, wound for wound, stripe for stripe" (Exod. 21:23–25).

Note that these passages are intended to be used by a court when a crime has been committed. They aren't instructions telling people to take personal revenge. The point of having a court system is to *prevent* people from doing that by seeing that justice is done when an innocent party is harmed.

If people take their own revenge, they may often do so excessively. A person who has been wounded or seen a loved one wounded may *kill* the perpetrator, for example. Courts exist to keep this from happening. To do their job properly, courts need to be seen as administering justice fairly. If they are too lenient, people may take matters into their own hands. Thus the "eye for an eye" passages. They direct courts to let the punishment fit the crime, which is a fundamental principle of justice. This principle promoted the common good and order of society by discouraging people from taking their own revenge.

In a world without an extensive prison system, this may have literally meant "an eye for an eye," though not always. Numbers 35:31 specifies that no ransom can be accepted in a case of murder, suggesting that in lesser cases the guilty party could pay compensation. A person thus might avoid "an eye for an eye" if he provided appropriate compensation to the injured party.

Justice can also be tempered by mercy in other ways. Thus Jesus counseled individuals to "turn the other cheek" rather than pressing for "an eye for an eye" justice (Matt. 5:38–39).

15. How can we resolve historical difficulties in the Old Testament?

Our knowledge of the ancient world is limited. Most events were never recorded in writing, and the records of many that were written down have been lost. Further, reports can conflict, with ancient authors disagreeing about exactly what happened on a particular occasion. This poses a challenge for historians in every field, and that includes scholars of biblical history.

Keeping a number of principles in mind can help resolve these difficulties. First, there is the incompleteness of our sources. Sometimes skeptics have accused the biblical authors of being in error because they mention something not recorded in extrabiblical sources. However, just because something isn't independently attested-to does not mean that it didn't happen. The accounts in the Old Testament themselves provide historical evidence for the events they describe, and this evidence cannot simply be dismissed.

Second, just because we may not presently have extrabiblical confirmation for an event does not mean we will not one day get it. As archaeology has developed, it has provided confirmation for biblical claims that were previously disputed. For example, skeptics at one time questioned whether the Israelites were around as early as the 1200s B.C. However, in 1896, the British archaeologist Sir Flinders Petrie discovered an Egyptian record, known as the Merneptah Stele, which documents the existence of the Israelites around 1210 B.C.

Third, in cases where the biblical and extrabiblical sources conflict, one cannot simply assume that the biblical sources are wrong. For example, Egyptian scribes studiously avoided portraying their pharaohs as losing battles. Consequently, we would expect Egyptian records either to omit or misrepresent the defeat that Pharaoh Neco II suffered at the hand of the Babylonian king Nebuchadnezzar in 601 B.C., whereas Jeremiah's reference to it would be accurate (Jer. 46:2).

Fourth, we need to be sensitive to the way that the ancients wrote history. The techniques used in different time periods vary, and we cannot expect ancient historians—biblical or otherwise—to write in a modern fashion. For example, ancient histories involved a greater degree of approximation than modern ones do (answer 5). There were no tape recorders, and so paraphrases and reconstructed conversations were expected in historical records. They were meant to convey the gist of what happened, but the details often were understood to be approximations.

Fifth, we need to be sensitive to the genres that the ancient authors employed (answer 4). This is particularly the case when we are dealing with accounts of events that would have occurred long before they were written down. In these cases, the authors necessarily had less information about the events, and so they needed to employ more approximation in recording them in narrative form.

Thus in 1950, Pope Pius XII wrote,

> The first eleven chapters of Genesis, although properly speaking not conforming to the historical method used by the best Greek and Latin writers or by competent authors of our time, do nevertheless pertain to history in a true sense, which however must be further studied and determined by exegetes; the same chapters . . . in simple and metaphorical language adapted to the mentality of a people but little cultured, both state the principal truths which are fundamental for our salvation, and also give a popular description of the origin of the human race and the chosen people (*Humani Generis* 38).

Sixth, we need to be careful about whether a text is even attempting to offer a literal account or whether it is employing some degree of symbolism. We have already seen that Genesis 1 is not meant to offer chronological information about how God created the world and instead uses a symbolic, topical way of organizing the work of the Creator (answer 11), and we've looked at the proposal made by some Church Fathers and modern authors that aspects of the conquest narrative are not meant to be taken literally (answer 13).

In some cases, entire books that might at first glance appear to be historical could turn out on closer reading to be something else. We've mentioned Judith as an example of that (answer 4), and Pope John Paul II stated, "The Books of Tobit, Judith, and Esther, although dealing with the history of the chosen people, have the character of allegorical and moral narrative rather than history properly so called."[6]

There are thus a variety of principles that need to be kept in mind when considering proposed historical difficulties involving the Old Testament. For resources dealing in depth with specific difficulties, see "Further Reading" at the end of this book.

16. Do the infancy narratives conflict or contain historical errors?

Sometimes skeptics have claimed that the infancy narratives found in Matthew 1–2 and Luke 1–2 contradict each other. For example, it is pointed out that Luke has Mary living in Nazareth before going to Bethlehem, whereas in Matthew they don't go to Nazareth until later. It has also been claimed that they contain historical errors, such as Matthew's mention of Herod's slaughter of boys in Bethlehem (Matt. 2:16) or Luke's mention of the enrollment that took place when Jesus was born (Luke 2:1–5).

All these difficulties are resolvable. First, the infancy narratives don't contradict each other. They fit together very well. Here's an interwoven narrative:

Initially, Gabriel appears to Zechariah to announce the birth of John the Baptist (Luke 1:5–25). A few months later, Gabriel appears to Mary in Nazareth to announce the birth of Jesus (Luke 1:26–38), and Mary goes to visit Elizabeth before returning to Nazareth (Luke 1:39–56). Then John the Baptist is born (Luke 1:57–80).

Around this time, Joseph is informed that Mary is pregnant. He plans to divorce her, but an angel tells him to continue the marriage (Matt. 1:18–23). The two begin cohabiting (Matt. 1:24). This would be in Nazareth, per Luke's account.

Because of the enrollment announced by Caesar Augustus, the Holy Family travels to Bethlehem (Luke 2:1–5), where Jesus is born (Matt. 1:25a; Luke 2:7). That night, the shepherds visit them (Luke 2:8–20). Around the same time, the Magi observe the star in their homeland (cf. Matt. 2:2, 9).

Eight days after birth, Jesus is circumcised and named (Matt. 1:25b; Luke 2:21), and after forty days he is presented at the temple (Luke 2:22–38).

At this point, the Holy Family either returns to Nazareth or remains in Bethlehem (which they did is not clear). If they returned to Nazareth, they continued to visit Jerusalem and their relatives in Bethlehem multiple times every year for the three annual pilgrimage feasts (Exod. 23:14–17; cf. Luke 2:41).

Between one and two years after the birth (cf. Matt. 2:16), the Magi arrive and are directed to Bethlehem, where they find the Holy Family (Matt. 2:1–11). They are warned in a dream to return to their country by a different route (Matt. 2:12). Also warned in a dream, the Holy Family flees to Egypt (Matt. 2:13–15) to avoid the Slaughter of the Innocents (Matt. 2:16–18).

When Herod the Great dies, the Holy Family returns to Israel (Matt. 2:19–21), but Joseph learns Herod Archelaus is ruling in Judea and so takes the family to Nazareth (Matt. 2:22–23).[7]

Regarding Herod's slaughter of Bethlehem's baby boys, it is claimed that this is a myth, as we don't have extrabiblical records of it happening. However, the Gospel of Matthew is *itself* a record, and it cannot simply be set aside.

Further, we would not expect surviving extrabiblical records to mention the event. Bethlehem was small (Mic. 5:2), and in Jesus' day its population was between 300 and 1,000. The number of males under two was likely no more than twenty-five to thirty; perhaps no more than six or seven.[8] Given the small scale of the event, most people outside of Bethlehem wouldn't have been aware of it.

We don't have any of Herod's court records, and what knowledge we have of his acts is spotty, being principally derived from the Jewish historian Josephus, who was born decades after Herod died. Although Josephus does briefly mention Jesus in a couple of passages, it is unlikely he would have mentioned a small event like the Slaughter of the Innocents, if he was even aware of it.

Despite this, the story fits what was known about Herod. During the latter part of his reign he became paranoid and obsessed with keeping power. He saw plots everywhere and consequently executed his favorite wife and three of his sons. Caesar Augustus allegedly quipped, "It is better to be Herod's pig than son"[9]—the joke being that, as a Jew, Herod wouldn't eat pork and his pig would be safe. Herod is also known to have ordered mass executions. As his own death approached, he had a large number of prominent men confined in a stadium and ordered that they be killed so every family would grieve upon his death.[10]

The Slaughter of the Innocents is precisely what we would expect of Herod upon learning a baby was born who had a rival claim to the Jewish throne.

Concerning Luke's enrollment, claims are made that it wouldn't have been empire-wide, Joseph wouldn't have gone to Bethlehem, and Mary wouldn't have accompanied him. However, there are solutions to each challenge.

Augustus was emperor from 27 B.C. to A.D. 14, and he began the practice of empire-wide census taking: "Every five years, the Romans enumerated citizens and their property to determine their liabilities. *This practice was extended to include the entire Roman Empire in 5 B.C.*"[11] Because of the size of the empire, census taking was done in stages, taking place in different countries in different years. The decree of 5 B.C. thus likely wasn't implemented in Palestine for a few years. If the census was being done for tax purposes—as was normal—it would explain why Joseph returned to Bethlehem: he was from there and still had property there.

However, the enrollment may not have been a census. It may be an event that took place in 3–2 B.C. when the people of the empire swore allegiance to Augustus. In this case, Joseph may have returned to Bethlehem because Israel was organized tribally, and the Romans may have used the tribal structure to ensure that the locals took the oath. Since Bethlehem was the ancestral home of Joseph's clan, that is where he went.

Mary went with Joseph because she was his wife and could be better cared for by him and other relatives in Bethlehem than if left at home. Contrary to popular depictions in art, we need not suppose that she made the journey to Bethlehem in the last stages of pregnancy.

Luke merely says that "while they were there, the time came for her to be delivered" (Luke 2:6).

Finally, Luke and his readers were familiar with the way such enrollments worked. They had taken part in such events themselves. Even critical scholar Raymond Brown notes, "It is dangerous to assume that [Luke] described a process of registration that would have been patently opposed to everything that he and his readers knew."[12]

17. Does the Passion narrative contain contradictions or historical errors?

Various claims have been made regarding the narrative that chronicles the events that led up to Jesus' crucifixion. It has been asserted that the Gospels contradict each other regarding the day and time of the Crucifixion and that events like the release of Barabbas would not have occurred.

Regarding the day on which Christ was crucified, all four Gospels indicate it was a Friday, which was then known as the *Day of Preparation*—that is, the day on which people cooked food and made other preparations since they would not be allowed to work on Saturday—the Sabbath—which began at sundown (Matt. 27:62, Mark 15:42, Luke 23:54, John 19:31, 42).

The point that is disputed is the relationship of this Friday to the feast of Passover. The synoptic Gospels

(Matthew, Mark, and Luke) indicate that Jesus celebrated the Last Supper as a Passover meal (Matt. 26:19, Mark 14:16, Luke 22:13, 15). Since he was crucified on the afternoon of the following day, this would place the Crucifixion on the same day by Jewish reckoning—that is, on the day of Passover.

However, some claim that John places the Crucifixion at the same time the lambs were being slaughtered at the temple in preparation for the Passover feast, and he says the Jewish authorities did not want to enter Pilate's headquarters "so that they might not be defiled, but might eat the Passover" (John 18:28). This would suggest Jesus was crucified the day *before* the Passover meal was eaten.

There are multiple solutions to this difficulty. One of them consists of two points: first, John *never* says Jesus was crucified when the lambs were being slaughtered. This myth is so commonly repeated that people think it's in the Bible when it is not.

Second, the reason that the Jewish authorities didn't want to defile themselves was because Passover continued for a week after the lamb was eaten (Exod. 12:15, 18–20), and they wanted to *continue* to eat sanctified food during the festival.

John thus does not contradict the synoptics' indication that Jesus was crucified on the first day of Passover, following the eating of the Passover lamb the previous evening.

Regarding the time of day, Mark says Jesus was crucified at "the third hour" (Mark 15:25), and all three synoptics record the darkness from "the sixth hour" to "the ninth hour" while he was on the cross (Matt. 27:45; Mark 15:33; Luke 23:44), but John indicates that Jesus wasn't yet crucified at "the sixth hour" (John 19:14).

The solution is straightforward: in first-century Judaea, the custom was to count twelve hours from sunrise, as illustrated in Jesus' parable in Matthew 20:1–16, where a man hires workers at the third, sixth, ninth, and eleventh hours of daytime.

John, however, was using the Roman practice of counting hours beginning at midnight. Thus in John 1:39 two disciples are said to spend "that day" with Jesus, even though they met him "about the tenth hour." This would make sense if John were counting from midnight (making the tenth hour 10 a.m.) but not if he was counting from dawn (making the tenth hour 4 p.m.).

The timing of the Crucifixion thus is clear if we take account of the two systems of reckoning hours. In John, Pilate brings Jesus out to the crowd at "about the sixth hour" after midnight (around 6 a.m.). According to Mark he is then crucified at "the third hour" after dawn (around 9 a.m.). And according to all three synoptics, darkness covered the land from the sixth to the ninth hours after dawn (from around noon to 3 p.m.).

As to the release of Barabbas, we do not have an extrabiblical record that says, "Pilate customarily released a prisoner at Passover," but that's hardly surprising. Releasing a prisoner at the Jewish capital on a Jewish feast would be a purely local custom, and we don't have detailed records of the Roman administration in Judaea.

However, leaders often pardon popular political prisoners to curry favor with their subjects. We have records of ancient rulers in Judaea doing just that. Both Herod Archelaus (4 B.C.–A.D. 6) and the Roman governor Albinus (A.D. 62–64) did so.[13] And the Jewish *Mishnah* (a collection of oral traditions) contains provisions for slaughtering the Passover lamb for prisoners released at Passover.[14]

Even if we didn't know all that, the Gospels are historical records in their own right, they must be taken seriously, and *all four* mention the custom (Matt. 27:15; Mark 15:6; Luke 23:18; John 18:39).

18. How can we deal with the differences in the Resurrection narratives?

Critics have pointed to differences in the Gospel accounts of what happened after Jesus' resurrection and charged them with contradicting each other. However, this is not the case.

St. Paul indicates that Jesus made multiple postresurrection appearances (1 Cor. 15:5–8), and Luke indicates that Jesus appeared repeatedly over a period of forty days (Acts 1:3). Consequently, the evangelists needed to make choices about what appearances to include in their Gospels.

The solutions to the proposed difficulties become apparent when we recognize the different choices the authors made in selecting and sequencing their material (answers 6 and 7). Here is an interwoven narrative:

All four Gospels agree that women went to Jesus' tomb after the Sabbath, around dawn on the first day of the week (Matt. 28:1; Mark 16:1–2; Luke 24:1; John 20:1). The stone was rolled away, the body was gone, and they encountered an angel (Matt. 28:2–7; Mark 16:4–7; Luke 24:2–7, 10; John 20:1, 11–13).

The evangelists vary in which details they mention. All four indicate that Mary Magdalen was among the women, while Matthew, Mark, and Luke also mention her companions. Which companions they mention is presumably determined by whom they wanted to emphasize.

Matthew mentions there were guards at the tomb (Matt. 27:62–66; 28:4, 11–15). He also records that an angel rolled back the stone. Matthew thus makes explicit something that is implicit in the other three accounts. The way he records the angel's action could be read as a flashback (to what happened before the women arrived). Even without this reading, the evangelists were not bound to record events in chronological order.

Matthew and Mark mention one angel, whereas Luke and John mention two. The evangelists record different parts of the angels' message. Matthew and Mark mention that Jesus will appear to the disciples in Galilee, whereas Luke and John omit this.

John mentions that between the time the women first visited the tomb and the angelic encounter, Peter and John visited the tomb (20:2–10). Peter's visit is also confirmed in Luke 24:12. John also mentions the appearance of Jesus to Mary Magdalen (20:14–17), and Matthew and Mark indicate that Jesus appeared to the other women (Matt. 28:9–10, Mark 16:9).

Luke mentions appearances Jesus made the same day in the Jerusalem vicinity (Luke 24:13–44), whereas Matthew chose one in Galilee (Matt. 28:16–20). Mark also indicates Jesus appeared in Galilee (Mark 14:28; 16:7), but his original ending (which may be paralleled in Matthew) appears to have been lost. John records post-resurrection appearances in both Galilee and Jerusalem (John 20:19–29; 21:1–23).

After visiting Galilee, the disciples were back in the Jerusalem area before the Ascension (Luke 24:50–53, Acts 1:9–12), and on this occasion Jesus told them to remain in the city until the descent of the Holy Spirit on Pentecost, when they began their major evangelistic work (Luke 24:49, Acts 1:4; 2:1–47).

This is the reason Luke focuses on the appearances in and around Jerusalem. He is planning to chronicle, in Acts, how the Christian faith began spreading in stages, "in Jerusalem and in all Judea and Samaria and to the end of the earth" (Acts 1:8). Pulling the literary focus away from Jerusalem to Galilee would distract from the events he will chronicle in Acts.

Matthew and Mark, not planning on writing sequels to their Gospels, focused on an appearance in Galilee, bringing closure on a literary level by taking us back to where Jesus' ministry began. And John, writing to supplement the synoptic Gospels, records additional appearances in both places.[15]

19. Do James and Paul contradict each other?

As in the famous story of blind men trying to describe an elephant based on individual parts they have touched, individual human beings are only capable of grasping part of the infinite mystery of God. The authors of the Bible thus have their own theological approaches and themes that they emphasize.

Sometimes the differences in how they express themselves, including the way they use terms, can generate Bible difficulties. Perhaps the most famous involves statements made by St. James and St. Paul on the topic of justification.

James famously says, "You see that a man is justified by works and not by faith alone" (James 2:24), whereas Paul says, "We hold that a man is justified by faith apart from works of law" (Rom. 3:28), and, "A man is not justified by works of the law but through faith in Jesus Christ" (Gal. 2:16).

Paul's teaching was widely misunderstood (Rom. 3:8; cf. 2 Pet. 3:15–16), and it is possible that James had encountered distorted reports of what Paul was teaching and decided to clarify matters. However, a careful reading shows he is not contradicting Paul. In actuality, the two are using key terms—faith, works, and justification—in different senses.

First, regarding the Greek term for faith/belief, James uses it to refer to intellectual assent to the truths about God. Thus he says, "You believe that God is one; you do well. Even the demons believe—and shudder" (James 2:19). But Paul refers to what theologians call "formed faith" or "faith formed by charity." Thus he says what counts is "faith working through love" (Gal. 5:6).

Second, regarding works, James uses this term to refer to positive actions flowing from belief in God—good works—such as giving food and clothing to the needy (James 2:15–16) or the actions performed by Abraham and Rahab in God's service (James 2:23, 25).

In Paul's key passages, however, he refers not to "works" but to "works of the law"—works done because they're required by the Law of Moses. He thus sees works of the law as characteristic of Jews but not Gentiles (Rom. 3:28–30; Gal. 2:11–16), and the main work he is concerned with is the Jewish initiation ritual of circumcision (Rom. 2:25–29, 3:30; Gal. 5:6, 6:13–15).

Third, James and Paul are discussing different kinds of justification. Scripture indicates that there is more than one form of this. In addition to the justification that occurs when we first come to God and are forgiven, there is an ongoing growth in righteousness throughout the Christian life.

Thus James refers to Abraham as being justified when he offered Isaac on the altar (James 2:21). This occurred in Genesis 22, long after Abraham was initially justified. Indeed, he had been explicitly pronounced righteous/justified as early as Genesis 15:6.

However, Paul is principally concerned with initial justification—the kind that occurs when we first come to God. Thus he speaks of justification in the context of Christian conversion (1 Cor. 6:9–11, Gal. 2:16), and he stresses that Christians do not need to observe the Law of Moses or be circumcised (cf. Gal. 5:4, 6:15).

James thus holds that intellectual faith alone does not save and that our ongoing growth in righteousness *after* conversion is furthered by doing good works. Paul, on the other hand, holds that if we have faith working through love then we have been forgiven and do not need to be circumcised and keep the Law of Moses to be justified (either at the beginning of the Christian life or afterward).

We thus find the two authors expressing complementary—not contradictory—views.

20. What is the Bible's attitude toward women?

There is no doubt that attitudes toward women were very different in ancient times compared to today. This has led some to propose Bible difficulties on the subject, sometimes charging that the Bible is misogynistic and that it fundamentally devalues women.

Space does not allow us a detailed survey of passages involving women, but several general points need to be made. First, because of the age in which the Bible was written, it is natural that its authors would write in terms of their own culture and the roles that women played in the society of their day.

Second, as we noted earlier (answer 9), we must be careful to identify the author's attitude toward the subject under discussion. For example, Deuteronomy 21:10–14—which deals with taking as wives women captured in battle—is actually meant to restrain the lust of their captors and to provide protections for the women, who, the text says, have been "humiliated" (v. 14).

Third, Bible passages—including those regarding women—must be read in terms of the stage of progressive revelation that had been reached (answer 10). This particularly affects Old Testament passages, which were written before God's definitive revelation of his will in Jesus Christ.

God initially took the Israelites for himself as a people when they were at a very low stage of religious and spiritual development. They were even worshipping idols at the time God led them out of slavery in Egypt (Lev. 17:7, Deut. 32:17), and it took a centuries-long process for God to educate them spiritually and wean them away from pagan practices.

Jesus indicated that, while this process was underway, God tolerated certain practices on account of Israel's hard-heartedness, and the way women were treated in the Old Testament certainly falls under that heading.

Fourth, God eventually brought about the definitive revelation of his will in Christ (cf. Heb. 1:1–2, Jude 3). Despite the low social status of women in the first century, Jesus freely associated with and showed compassion for women (e.g., Mark 5:25–34, Luke 7:11–17, 13:10–17), and he counted women among his key disciples (Luke 8:2–3).

Indeed, the New Testament depicts women as among his most faithful disciples, witnessing his crucifixion and burial and coming to anoint his body after death, while the male disciples had fled (Matt. 26:31) and were in hiding (John 20:19). This is why the women were privileged to be the first witnesses of the Resurrection (Matt. 28:9–10, Mark 16:9, John 20:14–17).

Jesus showed high regard for his mother, and it was she who convinced him to perform his first public sign

(John 2:1–11); he made provision for her care after his death (John 19:26–27); the New Testament describes her as the most blessed of women (Luke 1:42); and in the Catholic view she is the most blessed person of either sex (CCC 967, 1172).

Fifth, there are differences between men and women. This is obvious from the fact that they are different sexes, though some moderns have sought to minimize these to the point of denying them and any implications they may have for the roles men and women most naturally fulfill in society. This is an area in which modern attitudes should not simply be uncritically accepted. Whatever natural differences in gender roles may exist, though, do not imply an inequality of the sexes.

Finally, the Bible recognizes the fundamental equality of men and women, and it does so from the very beginning. Thus the *Catechism* notes,

> God created man and woman together and willed each for the other. The word of God gives us to understand this through various features of the sacred text. "It is not good that the man should be alone. I will make him a helper fit for him" (Gen. 2:18). None of the animals can be man's partner. The woman God "fashions" from the man's rib and brings to him elicits on the man's part a cry of wonder, an exclamation of love and communion: "This at last is bone of my bones and flesh of my flesh" (Gen.

2:23). Man discovers woman as another "I," sharing the same humanity (371).

God thus created men and women "to be a communion of persons, in which each can be 'helpmate' to the other, for they are equal as persons ('bone of my bones') and complementary as masculine and feminine" (CCC 372).

The text of Genesis thus indicates that women, like men, are made in the image of God: "God created mankind in his image; in the image of God he created them; male and female he created them" (Gen. 1:27, NABRE; cf. CCC 369). The fundamental equality of men and women in God's eyes is expressed even more clearly in the New Testament, which proclaims, "There is neither Jew nor Greek, there is neither slave nor free, there is neither male nor female; for you are all one in Christ Jesus" (Gal. 3:28).

Further Reading

Akin, Jimmy. *A Daily Defense: 365 Days (Plus One) to Becoming a Better Apologist.*
—. "How the Accounts of Jesus' Childhood Fit Together." JimmyAkin.com.
—. "How the Resurrection Narratives Fit Together." JimmyAkin.com.
Archer, Gleason. *New International Encyclopedia of*

Bible Difficulties. Zondervan, 2001.

Blomberg, Craig. *The Historical Reliability of the New Testament.* Nashville: B&H Academic, 2016.

Horn, Trent. *Hard Sayings: A Catholic Approach to Answering Bible Difficulties.* El Cajon: Catholic Answers Press, 2016.

Finegan, Jack. *Handbook of Biblical Chronology* (2nd ed.). Hendrickson Pub, 2015.

Hoffmeier, James. *Israel in Egypt: Evidence of the Authenticity of the Exodus Tradition.* New York: Oxford University Press, 1999.

—. *Ancient Israel in Sinai: The Evidence for the Authenticity of the Wilderness Tradition.* New York: Oxford University Press, 2011.

Kaiser, Walter, et al. *Hard Sayings of the Bible.* Downers Grove: InterVarsity Press, 2010.

Kitchen, Kenneth. *On the Reliability of the Old Testament.* Grand Rapids: Eerdmans, 2006.

Pontifical Biblical Commission. *The Inspiration and Truth of Sacred Scripture.*

Ramage, Matthew. *Dark Passages of the Bible: Engaging Scripture with Benedict XVI & Thomas Aquinas.*

Steinmann, Andrew. *From Abraham to Paul: A Biblical Chronology.* Saint Louis: Concordia Publishing House, 2011.

About the Author

Jimmy Akin is an internationally known author and speaker. As the senior apologist at Catholic Answers, he has more than twenty years of experience defending and explaining the Faith.

Jimmy is a convert to the Faith and has an extensive background in the Bible, theology, the Church Fathers, philosophy, canon law, and liturgy. Jimmy is a weekly guest on the national radio program Catholic Answers Live, a regular contributor to *Catholic Answers Magazine,* and a popular blogger and podcaster. His books include *The Fathers Know Best* and *A Daily Defense.* His personal website is JimmyAkin.com.

Endnotes

1   *Letters* 82:1:3.

2   General Audience, January 29, 1986.

3   Pontifical Biblical Commission, *The Inspiration and Truth of Sacred Scripture,* 127.

4   *Summa Theologiae* I-II:94:5 reply to obj. 2.

5   Pontifical Biblical Commission, *The Inspiration and Truth of Sacred Scripture,* 127.

6   General Audience, May 8, 1985.

7   For more, see "How the Accounts of Jesus' Childhood Fit Together" at JimmyAkin.com.

8   Paul Maier, "Herod and the Infants of Bethlehem," in *Chronos, Kairos, Christos II.* Jerry Vardaman, ed. 177-178.

9   Macrobius, *Saturnalia* 2:4:2.

10 Josephus, *Antiquities of the Jews* 17:6:5-6.

11 "Census," in *Encyclopedia Britannica,* 2016 ed., emphasis added.

12 *The Birth of the Messiah,* 549.

13 Josephus, *Antiquities* 17:8:4[204-205], 20:9:5[215].

14 *m. Pesahim* 8:6.

15 For more information, see "How the Resurrection Narratives Fit Together" at JimmyAkin.com.

Become part of the team.
Help support Catholic Answers.

Catholic Answers is an apostolate dedicated to serving Christ by bringing the fullness of Catholic truth to the world. We help good Catholics become better Catholics, bring former Catholics "home," and lead non-Catholics into the fullness of the Faith.

Catholic Answers neither asks for nor receives financial support from any diocese. The majority of its annual income is in the form of donations from individual supporters like you.

To make a donation by phone using your credit card, please speak with one of our customer service representatives at 888-291-8000.

To make a donation by check, please send a check payable to "Catholic Answers" to:

> Catholic Answers
> 2020 Gillespie Way
> El Cajon, CA 92020

To make a donation online, visit **catholic.com**.

Catholic Answers

TO EXPLAIN & DEFEND THE FAITH

catholic.com